indoor PLANT
DÉCOR

indoor PLANT DÉCOR

The Design Stylebook for Houseplants

Kylee Baumle ◆ Jenny Peterson

st. Lynn's press

PITTSBURGH

Indoor Plant Décor
The Design Stylebook for Houseplants

ISBN-13: 978-0-9855622-0-5

Library of Congress Control Number: 2012940819
CIP information available upon request

First Edition, 2013

St. Lynn's Press . POB 18680 . Pittsburgh, PA 15236
412.466.0790 . www.stlynnspress.com

Book design–Holly Rosborough
Editor–Catherine Dees

Photo credits:
Photos by the authors appear on pages vi, x, xi, xii, xiv, 2, 4-13, 15, 17 (top r.), 20-27, 29, 31, 36, 37, 41, 43 (top), 45, 49 (cups), 50, 52, 54-56, 58, 61, 65-67, 68 (top l.), 69-71, 73 (top, bottom r.), 74, 77, 79, 81, 83, 84 (r.), 85-91, 92 (styleboard), 98, 102, 103, 104 (l.), 105-107, 110-113, 114, 115-117, 119-123, 128, 130, 132 (bottom), 134, 136, 142.

Front cover: (top l.) author photo; (bottom l.) okeyphotos; (r.) author photo

Back cover: Laura Eubanks/Design for Serenity

Other photo credits are listed on page 139.

Printed in Canada
on certified FSC recycled paper using soy-based inks

This title and all of St. Lynn's Press books may be purchased for educational, business, or sales promotional use. For information please write:
Special Markets Department . St. Lynn's Press . POB 18680 . Pittsburgh, PA 15236

10 9 8 7 6 5 4 3 2 1

To Kara, who encouraged me to share
my love of gardening through words.

Kylee

❧

To Julie, who showed me the ropes;
to Dr. Carlos Rubin De Celis, who encouraged me
to live my life during cancer treatment; and
most of all, to Brett, who gently pushed me forward
when my feet wouldn't move.

Jenny

Bromeliad

TABLE OF CONTENTS

EIGHT DÉCOR STYLES

Introduction

It used to be that indoor gardening meant a ficus tree in the corner of the living room, a pothos plant trailing from the top of the entertainment center and a row of African violets in the kitchen window. While we wouldn't knock any plant that thrives in indoor conditions, contemporary gardening has moved far beyond the expected and traditional houseplant. Add to that the myriad of interior décor styles, and it becomes difficult to know just how to use houseplants as a part of your home's overall design scheme. That's where we come in. In our book we show you how to define your personal décor style, and then guide you into making stylish plant, container and accessory choices to pull it all together.

We aim to inspire you to create green interiors that utilize new plants, cutting-edge displays and fresh container ideas for every area of your home – from charming vignettes and snappy contemporary displays to entire garden rooms. Consider this your one-stop, "to-the-minute" stylebook.

If there's one thing we hear most often about houseplants, it's, "I just can't grow them." We understand. Gardening is a lifelong learning experience and to be honest, we weren't very good at keeping plants alive when we first started out either. In *Indoor Plant Décor*, we'll give you some basic tips to help you grow houseplants successfully, because you can't use them as design elements in your home if you can't keep them alive, right? And we assure you, there are some easy and beautiful plants out there that you can use to decorate your home.

The two of us come from vastly different backgrounds. Kylee lives on an acre in rural Northwest Ohio, while Jenny recently moved from an apartment with a balcony garden to a full acre in urban Austin, Texas. So not only are our own homes and gardens different in style, they exist in widely differing growing zones and climates. These realities are important considerations for all of us when making plant choices, as they affect what is available to us where we live. With that in mind, we'll be making suggestions for both plants

and materials that are relatively easy to find, no matter where you live (albeit with the occasional challenging-to-find but oh-so-worth-it treasure).

Jenny owns her own landscape design business and brings a design sensibility to the table, while Kylee focuses on the how, why, and where of growing the plants. What we have in common is our love of gardening and our desire to share practical yet stylish ways of using these living elements as part of home décor – and not just as an afterthought.

The mission of *Indoor Plant Décor* is to improve your confidence in choosing plants that fit your design style as well as your lifestyle. We hope you will benefit from our own adventures into the wonderful world of houseplant design. We know the amazing power plants have to transform an interior environment – even our state of mind.

Perhaps you'll like an idea shown here and you'll use it just as it's presented. Or maybe what you see will spark another idea that works better in your particular situation. We'd love to hear how you've used our book to enhance your home; and even better, if it has inspired you to try your hand for the first time at growing beautiful plants right where you live.

Kylee Baumle • Jenny Peterson

What's Your Style?

Wouldn't it be nice if you could just put your finger on the exact style of décor you like? The truth is, most of us can't do that because we like this from that style and that from this style…and just what do you call *that?* Eclectic, maybe, and that's a style too. In fact, it's one of the chapters in our book. It's probably one of the easiest décors to pull together, but there's so much more.

Let's take a look at this from a practical point of view. We generally like to surround ourselves with those things that make us most comfortable – that evoke a cozy, warm feeling. When we walk into our home, we want to feel like we're home. So it goes to figure that we gather furniture and design objects that do that for us. Sometimes it's with intention and other times things seem to just fall in our laps when we least expect them.

We draw on our past and the good from it. We live in the present and choose from those things we enjoy at the moment. We look to the future and

Baby's tears

include our dreams as reminders of what may come. All of these contribute to the individuals we are – and they will influence our design choices as well.

You'll notice throughout the book that we feature conventional, logical design combinations as well as some quirky, fun ensembles. What works in your home may not appeal to your neighbor. But you never know what will become the inspiration for your own version of what you see here.

To keep your home from becoming chaotic and confusing, it helps to define the style that you call your own and to keep that in mind when you're out and about, meandering through the aisles at your favorite stores. That's not to say that you can't include a random item in your decorating scheme that doesn't seem to fit; sometimes whimsy adds just the right touch. But if you want to keep to a particular style, don't overdo it. We'll show you what we mean.

We will be featuring eight design themes, with names like *Peaceful Zen* and *Vintage Vibe* – each with its own chapter, photo examples, plant list, tips and how-to's. The next best thing to having us in for tea and a personal consultation!

Beyond style: the health bonus

Besides the aesthetic benefits, houseplants are good for our physical well-being. We know that all plants exchange carbon dioxide for oxygen, but many of them take it one step further and purify the air of toxins. Houseplants that multitask! We've indicated in the plant chart on pages 126-128 which ones are capable of this. Even people with allergies can benefit from growing these hardworking air purifiers in their homes. Just one more reason we love them.

How to use this book

Each chapter starts with a styleboard of images, showing a representation of what we consider to be that particular style. Following a descriptive introduction, we suggest plants that work by virtue of their architectural footprint, ease of care, sense of place, colors and patterns – or any combination of these. As you go along, you'll see that a number of plants work with more than one décor. And for those of you who enjoy taking a real hands-on approach to things, each chapter comes with a fun and easy, step-by-step DIY project.

A dramatic planting that holds
its own with a bold interior

And don't worry — we won't leave you stranded when it comes to plant choices and care. Through-out the book, you'll find plant suggestions and basic tips on how to keep your plants looking good. In the *Practical Matters* chapter, there's information about the care and feeding of your plants — and a quick-reference plant chart to help you pair them up with your growing and maintenance preferences. Want only easy-care plants? Willing to put up with some plant divas? Depending on your degree of commitment to care, you'll find something for all levels.

Primrose

For more detailed information on all of the above, check out the resources listed in the back; we've left suggestions for additional reading and a list of some of the manufacturers and vendors for many of the plants, containers and other accoutrements featured in the book.

Although design and aesthetics will always be subjective, we invite you to join our ongoing conversation about how houseplants can transform your home, apartment or dorm room. No matter how large or small your space or your budget, chic and creative indoor plant décor can be yours.

Let's get started!

Classic Elegance

For those who love the finer things in life, their home is their castle — literally. Okay, so it might not be Downton Abbey, but it is arrayed in a way that speaks of the so-called good life. Though the words classic and elegant may give the impression of wealth, you don't have to spend a king's ransom to surround yourself with beautiful formal furnishings.

Velvets and brocades are appropriate textures, and curvy lines are right at home. Crystal, silver, and mercury glass are beautiful elements that add a touch of class. The only thing that might be easier than finding elegant furniture and fabrics, if you choose this style, is finding plants that go with it.

First steps

You really can spend as little or as much as you want and still have a home that exudes elegance. Off-price retail stores such as T.J. Maxx and Home Goods provide us with the opportunity to acquire lovely decorator items at minimal cost. You'll find plenty of appropriate containers for your plants in stores like these, too.

Some plants have an elegant feel to them by virtue of their form. Ferns, for example, bring grace and sophistication to any room. Large-leaved plants such as some philodendrons and palms give the illusion of prosperity and command respect as floor plants, especially when used in pairs.

Few plants fit the profile of classic and elegant like an orchid. Don't cringe, thinking you can't grow them, because even a simple and accessible *Phalaenopsis* (moth orchid) likes the same type living conditions we do. Their refined blooms are awe-inspiring and can last for months.

Orchid

Amaryllis

Plants don't always need to be potted in order to add a dimension of elegance; in fact, cut flowers are a quick and inexpensive way to change up a look according to seasons, and there's no shortage of urns and vases in crystal and glazed finishes.

Be adventuresome and try some unusual or unexpected plants like succulents or tillandsias — but be sure to pair them with sophisticated containers that have glamorous appeal, like silver or glass.

Tillandsias

4

Classic planting with a whimsical twist

Plants for a Classic Elegance Interior

These plants have a regal silhouette, giving your décor a touch of class:

Snake plant

African violet (*Saintpaulia ionantha*)

Bromeliads

Clivia (*Clivia miniata*)

Desert rose (*Adenium obesum*)

Ferns

Ivies

Jade plant (*Crassula ovata*)

Norfolk Island pine
   (*Araucaria heterophylla*)

Orchids

Palms

Peace lily (*Spathiphyllum cochlearispathum*)

Peperomia (*Peperomia* spp.)

Philodendron (*Philodendron* spp.)

Rex begonia (*Begonia rex*)

Rubber tree (*Ficus elastica*)

Snake plant (*Sansevieria* spp.)

Succulents

Tillandsias

Details

For Classic Elegance, the containers you choose take on great importance, perhaps more so than for any other style. It's doubtful that a bohemian style of pot will appeal to you, but in the event that it does, this is not the place for mixing such containers with crystal or sterling silver. One or the other will not be believable and you'll just come across as not wearing the style well.

Here, you can lather on the luxe, and turn an ordinary container into something special, merely by use of a can of paint. Glorious faux finishes are no further away than your local home improvement store. There are spray paints that adhere to plastic, transforming inexpensive pots into elegant, glimmering containers that enhance not only your décor, but the plant contained within. Do be careful though, not to glam up *every* surface with bling or shine unless you are irresistibly drawn to an over-the-top look. A little can go a long way.

Family heirlooms can hold plants by serving as cachepots. Imagine a sterling silver soup tureen with a frilly fern or rambling ivy spilling out over the sides as a dining room centerpiece. Copper pots, while not inexpensive, will raise the aesthetic value of just about anything you put in them.

Wardian cases, once the darlings of Victorian homes, are again popular, and a unique way to showcase special plants. They help maintain a higher humidity level too, so think of filling them with plants that love those conditions, like ferns and orchids. They differ from terrariums in that plants are usually (not always) kept in their containers, rather than planted directly in the bottom of the Wardian case.

Classic and elegant can also be fairly minimal if you use a monochromatic color scheme in sophisticated colors. Aim for drama in the container shape or plant form, and keep accessories to a minimum.

Do This, Not That: **Be sure to keep plants trimmed of any yellowing or brown-edged leaves – and for goodness sake, don't hang on to plants that are clearly suffering. Nothing will bring down that beautiful classic elegance ambience like a half-dead plant.**

Step-By-Step: *Tabletop Water Garden*

Materials

A glass container: bowl, wide-mouth vase, etc.

Water plants such as taro, water lettuce, water hyacinth, duck weed, fairy moss etc.

Plastic pots shorter than the height of your glass vessel

Assorted rocks

Potting soil

Activated charcoal

Mosquito fish (optional)

Distilled water

1. Make sure your container is clean.
2. Line the bottom of the container with activated charcoal. Rinse the charcoal first to minimize darkening of the water by the charcoal.
3. Cover the charcoal with pebbles.
4. Fill the container with distilled water. Pour it in slowly to avoid dislodging the pebbles.
5. Plant your taro in a plastic pot with the potting soil, and cover soil surface with rocks.
6. Place the potted taro into the bottom of the container (nestled into the pebble layer) and add any floating plants, like water lettuce.
7. Carefully clean off the sides of the container, and remove any soil that has floated to the water surface.

Cheap Chic

First time interior gardeners, college kids in dorm rooms or anyone on a budget will appreciate the Cheap Chic way of inside gardening.

Or maybe you're new to the whole idea of designing with plants and you don't want to spend too much money initially. No matter what your situation, you still want to have chic and creative plant displays. There are lots of ways to accomplish your indoor garden on a budget; it just takes putting a little more time into thinking creatively, finding new and unusual ways of using plants, containers and accessories.

Having a Cheap Chic indoor garden does *not* mean you have to settle for lower quality or ugly materials. Tackiness is not an option! Have you ever heard that it doesn't take a lot of money to be fashionable? The same is true for your plants—know what you want and buy quality as you have the budget.

Start small. If you start small, your investment will be minimal. You can always add to a project or display as you go along. Think of it as "gardening on layaway" – you don't have to complete it all at once! A few ideas:

Start a plant collection. Some plants are a little pricey, or simply difficult to find. Know what type of plant you really love (are you drawn to quirky lithops, airy ferns, textural succulents or dramatic tropicals?) – and slowly add to your collection as you have the funds. The benefit, aside from the minimal investment, is that all your plants will have nearly the same care requirements, making maintenance a snap.

Boston fern

Purchase your large pieces first. These are the pieces that are typically more dramatic and give you more bang for your buck. You may have to save up a bit, but that oversized glazed container with a huge tropical plant or hearty fern in it will add instant drama to your living room or bedroom.

Focus on one area at a time. You may have a very small apartment or dorm room, and then your decision is an easy one because you have only a small area to work with. Group your plant display by your window or on your desktop, or hang a grouping of plants in a corner of your room. Use containers that are more colorful or interesting, so a small display will be noteworthy.

Buy plants that need some TLC. You can get some good deals on plants that need additional care to revive them. Cut back the dead/brown parts, repot them, give them some additional fertilizer and a good long drink to nurse them back to health. Ask your nursery staff to give you some tips — they are there to help you, and they want to move that inventory out.

Connect with plant people

Visit nurseries. Become friends with the staff of an upscale nursery or garden shop, and ask them to alert you to upcoming sales so you can buy quality. They won't do this for everybody, but they will for people they like and feel connected to. But remember — nobody likes a "cheapskate," so aim for friendly banter rather than wring-your-hands pleading.

Join garden groups. Many communities have garden clubs for either general gardening or special plants (The Succulent Society, Cactus Club or Orchid Society, for example) — joining these groups will afford you the option of annual plant swaps or monthly giveaways. The Master Gardeners often have plant sales, as do botanic gardens and wildflower centers. Look in your community newsletter or city's newspaper for notifications about upcoming sales. When participating in plant swaps or giveaways, it's not usually necessary to give every time you get, but do aim to balance the scales over time. Gardeners are generous people and love to share what they've grown, and they will appreciate when you reciprocate with them.

Plants for a Cheap Chic Interior

These plants should be readily available without busting your budget:

African violet *(Saintpaulia ionantha)*

Cacti

Cat palm *(Chamaedorea cataractarum)*

Croton *(Croton(Codiaeum variegatum)*

Dracaena *(Dracaena spp.)*

English ivy *(Hedera helix)*

Jade plant *(Crassula ovata)*

Kalanchoe *(Kalanchoe spp.)*

Kentia palm *(Howea forsteriana)*

Lady palm *(Rhapis excelsa)*

Living stones *(Lithops spp.)*

Peace lily *(Spathiphyllum cochlearispathum)*

Philodendron *(Philodendron spp.)*

Pothos *(Epipremnum aureum)*

Snake plant *(Sansevieria spp.)*

Spider plant *(Chlorophytum comosum)*

String-of-pearls *(Senecio rowleyanus)*

Tillandsias

String-of-pearls

Croton

Tillandsias

Shipping pallet
repurposed as a planter

Sources for inexpensive & creative containers

Home Improvement & Feed stores: Take a trip down the paint aisle and plumbing section of your home improvement store – really. You'll be surprised how many things you can find that you can plant in. Galvanized or tin buckets and troughs, PVC pieces and cinderblocks can all make interesting, inexpensive planters. While you're there, make sure you ask someone in the hardware department what you would need to drill drainage holes into solid pieces. These elements are perfect if you want a more industrial, streamlined feel to your indoor garden. Feed stores are a great resource for planters if you look for the small horizontal feed troughs – you can affix them to a wall for a creative vertical display.

Small feed troughs wrapped in burlap

Flea Markets: Scour flea markets, thrift stores and antique stores for vintage-y, offbeat ideas. Old cowboy boots, china teacups, vintage suitcases and cigar boxes can all be planted. Give yourself a budget of no more than $10, for example, per piece — and always remember that you can bargain for a better price in these types of stores. Don't worry about offending the vendor; they typically expect to be asked, "Is this your best price?" or "The tag says $20; can you do $10?" If you don't ask, you won't get!

Craft Stores: Craft and hobby stores are treasure troves for the creative mind — and perfect hunting grounds for people wanting one-of-a kind plantings. Look in the clearance sections as well as the seasonal décor aisles. Anything that can hold candles, potpourri or flowers can house plants. As with any object used as a container, pay attention to drainage and either make drainage holes or use plants that won't mind those conditions. And don't forget the moss: For a "no-container" planter, large amounts of bagged moss can support tillandsias. Simply hang the moss on a hook suspended from the ceiling and tuck your air plants in. Simple, cheap and chic!

Your Own Home: Take a tour through your basement, attic, kitchen and storage areas for little-used pieces that can be repurposed. Glass vases can be embellished with craft store finds, old toys can stand in as quirky planters and baskets can be turned into vertical

Tillandsias in hanging moss

wall "shelves" for an assortment of small plants. Or do you have some unattractive old containers that could use a style lift? Try wrapping them with items like quilt pieces, denim fabric, afghan sections or brightly colored reusable shopping bags. Or maybe you've got an old table that's seen better days and is just waiting for a touch of imagination.

Do This, Not That:

Inexpensive does not equal cheap, but it can be whimsical and unique. And if you are a DIYer as we are, make sure your craftsmanship is excellent. Nothing says tacky like a poorly executed homemade project! Clean up hot glue strands, weave in yarn ends and polish your old silver pieces.

Step-by-Step Project: *Cork Planter*

MATERIALS

Various wine corks
Drill bits (½" and ¼")
Small magnets (optional)
Craft glue

Small amount of potting soil
Tiny plant clippings (succulents are perfect)
Small amount of decorative aquarium gravel

1. Drill a pilot hole in the top of each cork with the smaller drill bit, then enlarge the hole with the larger bit, being careful to avoid drilling all the way through to the bottom. A hole 1" deep is perfect.

2. If you want to make the corks into refrigerator magnet planters, now is the time to glue a magnet onto the back of each cork. Otherwise, your cork planter will sit on a windowsill or tabletop.

3. Add a tiny amount of potting soil in the planting hole, then carefully place your plant clipping into the hole. Add more soil if necessary and gently tamp down to secure your clipping.

4. Add a tiny bit of aquarium gravel around the clipping to finish off your planting.

Water your cork planter with very small amounts of water (1 tablespoon or less) every 10 days or so, depending upon the type of plant you used. An eyedropper works well to get the water into the small opening. Eventually, you will have to transplant the clipping into a larger container to encourage it to grow and thrive.

PEACEFUL ZEN

Zen interiors happen when earthy elements meet up with a clean, contemporary vibe. These serene, peaceful places often feature neutrals with perhaps a pop of one striking color, strong architectural lines, simple furnishings and minimal embellishment. There is an emphasis on organic elements such as rock, earth and water – but rather than being of the granola variety, this organic sensibility is much more quietly sophisticated.

Accents like Buddha statuary, bamboo and bonsai are typically recognized in this interior style, but to keep your living room from looking too much like a "theme," use these elements sparingly and blend them with other less obvious design elements.

First Steps

Keep It Simple

If you already have a peaceful, zen-like interior – or are in the midst of creating one, but don't know where to start with your plantscaping – you're in luck. The motto in any Asian-inspired space is to keep it simple. Now, "simple" doesn't necessarily mean sparse, and it should not equal boring. Rather, zen spaces focus on eliminating clutter so that the items remaining create a sense of calm and balance, and truly reflect who you are. The fewer stimuli you have in your space, the more easily you can focus on those things that make you feel tranquil. Remember, clutter equals distraction in these types of spaces.

While you want your plant design to say "contemporary," avoid hopping on the newest trend or fad here. The Peaceful Zen interior garden is more timeless than trendy, more classic than here-today-gone-tomorrow. Acknowledge the here-and-now by making thoughtful plant and container choices rather than buying the latest product on the market — or take a trend like vertical gardening and pare it down from a tropical planted wall to a series of clean iron shelves or plant brackets.

Containers can range from glazed pottery to those with cool steel exteriors, or rough textures like wood or even concrete. In order to maintain unity, aim for containers with the same kind of "feel" (sleek or rough, warm or cool) rather than a disparate collection.

Banana

Use Statement Plants

In spaces like these, you want to use plants that create a commanding presence and make a statement. Aim for fewer, well-chosen plants rather than a jungle of messy collections. Plants with interesting textures, tall forms, large leaves and bold flowers will provide the dramatic yet clean and simple look you are seeking.

These plants can range from tropical to arid, large to small, but their forms will all be strong and definable.

Orchid

Palm

35

Plants for a Peaceful Zen Interior

Plants that have texture and bold yet clean lines:

Bonsai specimens

Cast iron plant (*Aspidistra elatior*)

Desert rose (*Adenium obesum*)

Dracaena (*Dracaena* spp.)

Jade plant (*Crassula ovata*)

Living stones (*Lithops* spp.)

Lucky bamboo (*Dracaena braunii*)

Mistletoe cactus (*Rhipsalis* spp.)

Orchids

Peace lily (*Spathiphyllum cochlearispathum*)

Philodendron (*Philodendron* spp.)

Sago palm (*Cycas revoluta*)

Snake plant (*Sansevieria* spp.)

Succulents

Tillandsias

ZZ plant (*Zamioculcas zamiifolia*)

Mistletoe cactus and tillandsias

Spanish moss and snake plant

Orchid

Devil's backbone

Chinese banyan

The Details

Color

While many zen-worthy plants are various shades of green, don't feel you are limited to only one color palette. Orchids come in a wide variety of hues and color patterns, and many succulents feature out-of-this-world blooms that are quite long lasting. Look for other foliage that is variegated with white, cream and burgundy edges or veins.

Containers can add a dose of color, but be careful what color you choose. Opt for one bold color and use it very sparingly, with more neutral shades in the background. No color is truly off limits, but there are particular hues of each color that work better than others in this type of interior. In general, avoid shocking hues like neon or primaries – but that being said, sometimes you have to know the "rules" before you knowingly break them, so use this guide as a starting place when making your own color choices.

Caladium

Whites, black, gray, chocolate and taupe are always good choices, and will blend with any color plant.

Reds — Russet, brick, sunset
Oranges — Burnt orange, apricot, dark orange-red
Yellows — Maize, mustard, ocher
Greens — Sage, olive, gray-green, chartreuse
Blues — Silver-blue, ink blue, slate blue, green-blue
Purples — Eggplant, amethyst, plum

Top: Bird's nest fern
Bottom: Moss

Elephant ear

Finishing Touches

The Peaceful Zen interior garden has touches of gravel, smooth river rock and textural mosses to offset the bold plant palette. Remember that this style is very organic in feel, and although it can also be highly sophisticated, that close-to-earth feeling should always remain intact. Use tiny gravel around succulents or cacti; tuck in handfuls of spongy reindeer moss under philodendrons or orchids. Smooth, chunky river rock can be puddled at the base of containers. And for ambiance, one well chosen water feature can

provide movement and sound. If you opt to add recognizable statuary, like Buddhas, choose one and make it bold. If you have the room, add a large moss-covered boulder – there is no reason why something so spectacularly dramatic should be relegated to the outdoors.

Do This, Not That:

Leave the fussy, frilly and frou-frou for another style, and forget about adding masses of tiny details that seem swarming to the eye. Be careful not to use too many iconic Asian symbols – like Buddhas, raked sand and lucky bamboo – which can make it look like you shopped the clearance aisle of the local imports store. Aim for bold and clean lines combined with sophisticated color palettes, rather than a high-contrast collection of hues.

Step-by-Step Project: *Kokedama or Japanese Moss Balls*

Materials
Small plant – African violets, pothos, ferns, succulents

Potting soil

Bonsai soil – available at bonsai supply stores or online

Sheet moss

Twine – optional, approximately 3 yards

Directions
1. Mix equal parts bonsai soil and potting soil.
2. Remove the plant from its pot and remove all the soil from around the roots.
3. Pat soil mixture around the roots of the plant, forming a ball or a teardrop shape.
4. Carefully press sheet moss onto the surface of the soil ball.
5. If you want to suspend your moss ball, wrap twine around the ball, knot it and hang it from a hook in the ceiling. Otherwise, set your moss ball in a saucer.

To water your moss ball, take it down from its hanger or remove it from its saucer. Soak it in water for about 5 minutes, allow it to drain, and replace it in its display. If you are using plants like succulents, they will need less water than ferns, so plan to water accordingly.

Staghorn fern

Vintage VIBE

There is something instantly comforting about vintage objects. The time-worn patinas, the soft fabrics, the classic colors and kitschy patterns – all remind us of a sense of history that is too quickly forgotten in a fast-paced world. Nothing is too perfect, too shiny or too matched. Vintage Vibe fuses all things old and nostalgic: mismatched or pieced-together fabrics, handmade items, homey fabrics and textures, and mixed-wood furniture.

But how to blend this style into one that says you're still current and hip? Nobody really wants to live in an antique store or Grandma's cottage, yet many of us love that aura of timelessness and quirkiness. Old and new can come together in a way that is soft and seamless, stylish and contemporary –

rather than stuffy and old. Your plant and container choices will reflect a person who values the past but has two feet firmly planted in the present. And isn't that the perfect place to be?

First Steps

USE old items in new ways. Vintage teacups and silver serving pieces can house trendy tillandsias and succulents; old books that are damaged can be turned into plant shelves for the DIYer.

Vintage leather case with ruffly begonia and prayer plant;
Echeveria

USE authentic pieces as accents. Your grandfather's old books or that charming collection of salt-and-pepper shakers can perfectly set off ferns and ivies in updated containers.

CHOOSE vintage-inspired pieces in fresh new colors. How about sweet little pots with splashes of shocking orange or offbeat purple?

OPT for retro colors in updated forms. Those vintage reds paired with turquoise or sage green are perfect for pottery when they come in sleeker, contemporary shapes.

USE "Grandma" plants in cool new ways. Remember your mother's African violets, or your grandmother's geraniums and Swedish ivies? Quaint plants are experiencing revivals in newer, modern containers and pots; square steel containers or those fashioned from clear glass all say "now."

Plants for a Vintage Vibe Interior

African violet *(Saintpaulia ionantha)*
Ferns
Ficus *(Ficus elastica)*
Ivies
Jade plant *(Crassula ovata)*
Philodendron spp.
Pothos *(Epipremnum aureum)*
Prayer plant *(Maranta leuconeura)*
Rubber plant *(Ficus elastic)*
Snake plant *(Sansevieria* spp.*)*
Spider plant *(Chlorophytum comosum)*
Succulents
Thanksgiving/ Christmas cactus *(Schlumbergera* spp.*)*
Tillandsias

Hen and chicks

Kalanchoe

Assorted succulents

The Details

Vintage spaces are charming and quirky, and are experiencing a revival with younger generations. It's somehow cool again to be using plants, décor and accessories that your grandma used, but take care to make design choices that update this look and keep it current. Make good use of "negative space" rather than cramming every antique find into your interior. It's possible to have a more minimalist vintage vibe if you choose just a few old pieces that have impact, while keeping everything else neutral and streamlined.

Try using newer, trendier plants like succulents or air plants that have a more modern look, and place them in older vessels; the contrast is immediately cool and new. Or, to give a jolt of fresh air, add a shocking color in neon hues to your planters. The idea is to mix and match the

old with new – whether it's with plants, containers or accessories – to bring your vintage plant display into the present day. Don't be afraid to experiment, as many vintage finds are very inexpensive (or free, if they come from your own attic or basement) and can be replaced, modified or moved around at will.

Another idea that we love is taking old, ho-hum planters and wrapping them with fabric to give an instant face-lift to your indoor garden. We've used placemats, decorative paper, old quilt and afghan pieces, fabric swatches and scraps – even table runners for larger containers. Simply wrap the container and overlap the ends in the back so the seam is invisible, pinning it if necessary, and then change it out as the mood strikes.

Do This, Not That

Vintage style can quickly seem old, stuffy and cluttered. When reusing old pieces for containers, be sure they are clean and in good repair. Dents and nicks are great; gaping holes and obvious tears and stains are not. Don't let your home and plant displays look junky. Allow for breathing room between pieces and slip in an occasional new piece to class up the joint.

Step-by-Step Project: *Terrarium*

Materials

Clear glass container, with or without lid, depending upon plant choice
Small plants, all with the same growing requirements. Plants in
    2-4" containers are best.
Activated charcoal, available at pet stores
Potting soil
Decorative sands in different colors (optional)
Small rocks
Decorative items – tiny statuary, driftwood, buttons, miniature animals
    or garden décor
Spray bottle w/water
Small funnel for neatly adding layers of materials
Chopsticks

1. Thoroughly clean your container.
2. Place a layer of pebbles on the bottom of the container for drainage.
3. Add a thin layer of activated charcoal to help keep soil fresh and absorb odors.
4. Layer sands over charcoal. (Steps 1-4 should equal about 1/3 the height of your container)
5. Add soil, being sure to create holes for each plant. If you have several decorative layers, be careful to leave the layers around the edges undisturbed, to maintain a clean look.
6. Place plants into the soil, and gently pack down around the roots to hold them

in place. Allow for some "negative space" around your plants; you don't want to pack the terrarium so full that the details are difficult to discern.

7. Add your decorative elements. Be creative but don't overdo it!

8. Use water from the spray bottle to gently clean the glass inside.

Maintenance

Water 1–2 times a week, moistening only the plants. Aim to keep the soil barely moist, but almost never bone-dry (depending upon plant selection). Humidity-loving plants will enjoy a closed container with a lid and misting several times a week. Keep your terrarium in natural, indirect light and avoid strong sunlight.

As with any planting anywhere, know the mature size of the plants you choose and match the container to the plants accordingly. Using too-large plants for a small vessel will lead to immediate overcrowding and plant health problems.

Plant Suggestions for Terrariums

For low light terrariums: mosses, ferns, baby's tears, *Sansevieria*, *Peperomia*

For high light terrariums (leave the lid off): cacti and succulents including jade, *Aloe*, *Echeveria*, *Sedum*

WORLD BEAT

ARE PEOPLE MORE WELL-TRAVELED THESE DAYS? It sometimes seems that way. Even if their budget doesn't allow for world travel, more and more people are becoming increasingly "worldly" in their perspective; so it should come as no surprise that their gardens and interior style would reflect that as well. If you love to showcase treasures from your travels, proudly display artifacts and fabrics from your trips abroad – or dedicate a part of your aesthetic to a future "dream trip" to a faraway place – you have a World Beat style.

This style infuses ethnic artwork with rich colors and textures, embellished accessories

Felt plant

and traditional fabrics and patterns. Your style could even be a fusion of several ethnic flavors, leading to a deeply layered and fascinating interior. Your plant choices will reflect the lands to which you've traveled, and the pots, containers and accessories will feature intricate and exotic details.

First Steps

Plant and Pot Pairings

When you're creating strong associations with different cultures, attention to detail is even more important. It's almost an art form to combine the right pot with the right plant, and then add the finishing touches to complete the display. If your interior tends to be very eclectic, combining design elements from all over the world, it's a good idea to have one thing that unites your décor (a very definable color palette, for example).

Here are some of the more common and recognizable décor styles from around the world:

- *The Tropics:* Sunny beach destinations are a favorite among travelers, and many people like to recreate that feeling of relaxation when they return home. Use plants with large foliage (philodendron, fiddle leaf fig tree, *Dieffenbachia*, palms) and those with tropical color (bromeliad,

Anthurium, *Alocasia*, bird of paradise, orchid). Oversized pots with strong forms are the way to go – either with golden bronze colors to let the plants shine, or with vivid tropical colors (orange, cobalt, apple green) to make a statement.

◆ *The Mediterranean:* These arid climates often feature drought-tolerant plants with bright colors and scented foliage and flowers, and pottery and accessories in sun-drenched hues. Think rich browns, intense cobalt blue, sea green, burnished orange and sandy neutrals. Style-spanning plants like palms and succulents are at home in this décor, as in several others – but it's here that aromatic herbs claim top billing. Plants like rosemary, oregano and lavender have long been associated with this region of the world, and with proper care, can flourish inside as well as out.

◆ *Mexico and Central America:* Think earthenware pots and textural cacti and succulents to show your love for the south-of-the-border, or if you're interested in making a statement, pair these plants with containers in fiesta colors of turquoise, orange or vivid cobalt blue. Traditional Talavera pottery is also in keeping with this region, with its brightly painted designs on brilliant glazed white backgrounds. Tillandsias (or air plants) and some tropical plants also define this region, as this part of the world can range from arid desert-like environments to lush semi-tropical forests.

Bird's nest fern

◆ *African:* This décor style features rich wood grains, neutral colors broken up with a single pop of color, organic themes and exotic accessories. Large architectural plants like philodendron, airy ficus trees and lacey fern-like plants are all at home in this style – but don't forget some oddball plants like lithops and tillandsias to complete your textural collection. Use wooden sugar molds, containers slipped into organic-feeling cachepots and curvy containers in burnished brown and golden hues to house your plants, and give a nod to animal life with an occasional zebra or leopard print.

◆ *Indian:* The exotic Indian subcontinent's style is marked by rich colors, jewel-toned accessories and embellishments, and by a wide range of plant material. Textiles are intricately textured and layered, creating a deeply alluring and sensual décor. Opt for an array of planters in jewel or earth colors, or with intricate patterns or artistic surfaces like mosaic or bead-encrusted. Plant choices can range from those with dramatic foliage and forms like palms, dracaenas and other tree forms, to airy ferns and textural succulents and tillandsias.

Plants for a World Beat Interior

Alocasia spp.

Anthurium spp.

Bromeliads

Cacti

Croton (*Codiaeum variegatum*)

Dracaena (*Dracaena* spp.)

Ferns

Ficus spp.

Ivies

Living stones (*Lithops* spp.)

Orchids

Palms

Panda plant (*Kalanchoe tomentosa*)

Philodendron (*Philodendron* spp.)

Pitcher plant (*Nepenthes* spp.)

Rex begonia (*Begonia rex*)

Rosemary (*Rosmarinus officinalis*)

Succulents

Tillandsias

ZZ plant (*Zamioculcas zamiifolia*)

Panda plant

Bromeliad

Tillandsias

The Details

Accessories and Finishing Touches

The best décors pay attention to details, creating more of a finished product and overall display, rather than a half-hearted attempt at style. Bring your houseplant display full circle by adding a variety of embellishments, from subtle to textural and dramatic. Always keep in mind the environment you are trying to create (ethnic, elegant, earthy, rustic, contemporary, etc.) and make your choices wisely from there.

- Table runners or placemats in the hues of your region can beautifully set off your container displays on horizontal surfaces like dining room tables, sofa tables, ottomans and side tables.

- Wall tapestries and artwork combined with vertical plantings (hanging pots, wall boxes and pocket plantings) create an interesting textural display.

- Top dressings on the soil surface of your containers make an artistic statement. Choose pea gravel, chunky river rocks or colored sands for your arid plants, like cacti and succulents, and opt for sphagnum moss,

Dumb cane

dimensional mood moss or colored mosses (black, bright green) to complement your more airy or leafy plants.

■ Accessories like geodes, statuary, candles and pottery bowls interspersed with potted plants pump up the worldly ethnic feel.

Do This, Not That

This décor style has instantly recognizable elements from around the world, but it also has some inherent risks. Don't fall into the trap of creating a theme park in your living room or bedroom – nobody really wants their interior space to look like a gigantic safari-gone-wrong or a Disneyland overload, do they? It's always best to imply a theme rather than hit your family and friends in the face with obvious clichés. Don't overuse iconic elements like animal prints, cowboy boots, Buddha heads or wooden shoes. One or two is enough, thank you.

Step-by-Step Project: *Container Necklace*

This is jewelry for your container, adding a bit of bling to a brilliantly glazed pot or a subtle earthenware container — simply choose the beads that reflect the culture you want to bring to your plantings.

Materials

28-gauge beading wire

An assortment of small glass beads – we like glass rather than plastic because the light reflects beautifully off the glass

Larger beads for the necklace "points"

Heavy-duty scissors to cut wire

Christmas ornament hooks

1. Measure the length of beading wire you will need. This depends upon the size of your container, and how far down you want the necklace to droop. Cut it longer than you think you will need; you can always shorten it later.

2. Bend one end of the wire about 3" from the end so the beads won't fall off as you string them.

3. String your beads onto the wire. Decide ahead of time if you want a defined pattern or a loose, random beading.

4. Take the ends of your beaded wire and twist them together, cutting off the excess wire.

5. Bend the ends of several Christmas ornament hooks into an arc, so that the larger end hangs off the lip of your pot and the smaller end serves as a hanger for the beaded wire.

6. Hang the hooks off the edge of your pot at even intervals, adjusting the hooks to fit tightly over the rim, and hang your beaded wire evenly on the hooks around your pot.

7. Now take about 3" of wire and string it through each of the larger beads, twisting the wire close to the top of the bead. Twist the ends of the wire around your beaded strand right at the point where the strand hangs down.

8. Cut off any excess wire or pinch it together – this wire is very pliable and easy to bend.

Traditional Mix

✦

IF YOU'RE NOT SURE WHAT YOUR DECORATING STYLE IS, CHANCES ARE IT'S WHAT WE CALL TRADITIONAL MIX. Not to be confused with "eclectic," this style is composed of comfortable pieces of furniture with unfussy lines. Wall décor is likely to be an assortment of artwork that evokes pleasant images of family and home, such as a collection of framed photos.

It's unlikely that the chairs and sofa and end tables were purchased as a set, yet they blend well together by having similar woods and fabrics. Plaids, stripes, solids and perhaps some florals are the fabric patterns of choice, and nothing is overly bold. A traditional style has a conservative feel, but isn't boring.

First steps

Containers: You might be overwhelmed by the selection available to you. Here, you can add a burst of color to a traditional round pot by choosing an accent color that fits with your décor. Don't be afraid to play with shapes; simply using a square container can give you an updated look.

Traditional plant selections are plentiful, but remember that you're using them to enhance your décor, not clutter it up or dominate it. With this style, the plants you choose will not be major players, but will fit in much as a decorative pillow does on the sofa.

Though the common varieties of traditional houseplants are readily available, the good news is that you can now find a wonderful selection of cultivated varieties of old favorites. For example, we're all familiar with the tall, dark green foliage of *Sansevieria*, or snake plant, with the yellow edge. But a shorter, pale green version, 'Moonlight', has the same horticultural needs, giving an entirely different look. And then there's *Sansevieria cylindrica*, which has an interesting three-dimensional form.

Traditional plant choices are to your mind what comfort food is to your stomach.

A stylish color echo between container and mottled bromeliad foliage

While these plants also work well with Vintage Vibe styles, here they take on a little more contemporary feel, by virtue of container choices and placement.

On the desk: Peace lily;
In the room divider: ZZ plant

Snake plant

Plants for a Traditional Mix Interior

Boston fern *(Nephrolepis exaltata)*
Coleus *(Solenostemon scutellarioides)*
Dracaena *(Dracaena* spp.*)*
Ficus *(Ficus* spp.*)*
Geraniums *(Pelargonium* spp.*)*
Jade plant *(Crassula ovata)*
Orchids
Palms
Philodendron
(Philodendron spp.*)*
Pothos
   (Epipremnum aureum)
Snake plant
   (Sansevieria spp.*)*
Spider plant
   (Chlorophytum)
   comosum)
Tillandsias
Umbrella plant
   (Shefflera arboricola)

Jade plant and aloe

Coleus

The Details

While it's tempting to incorporate everything you like into a "mix" type of decorating style, too much can be cluttery and sabotage the very mood you're trying to evoke. Think of what you would miss most if it weren't in your home every day – that's your decorating core – and try to keep extras to a minimum. If you seem to have a lot of favorites, you can trade things in and out for a different look – just not "everything up-front all the time."

You can do the same kind of trading with your plant containers, by using cachepots for your plants instead of planting them directly into the containers. Just doing this will further open up your choices, because you won't have to worry about drainage

holes. You can change the color according to seasons, or the shape just for a different look. Using top-dressing, such as mosses, will help hide the space between the
plant's pot and the container.

Do This, Not That: It's easy for traditional decorating to look ho-hum and dated, and few of us want to feel like we're living in The Brady Bunch house in the new millennium. Though basic lines of this style remain constant over the years, you can give things an updated look by your choice of color or fabric – and of course, plant container selection.

Step-by-Step Project: *Planted Book*

Materials

Hardcover books, new or vintage, more than 1½" thick
X-ACTO® knife
Ruler
Potting soil
Small bits of decorative moss or gravel
Small plants – succulents work well; the shorter and "flatter," the better.
  Look for those in 4" pots.
Waxed paper or plastic bag

1. Decide where inside the book you want the planting hole to be; the title page is a good choice. Choose a page towards the beginning of the book so the book will lay flat when planted.

2. Using the ruler, measure out a square or a rectangle on that page.

3. With the X-ACTO® knife and the ruler as a guide, begin cutting out a few pages at a time from the book.

4. Continue cutting pages from the book until you have made a planting hole about 1½" deep. Line the planting hole with waxed paper or plastic; this will keep the rest of the book from being damaged when you water.

5. Add some potting soil in the hole and carefully place the plants in the hole. Tamp soil down around the plants to keep them settled in.

6. Add moss, decorative sand, or small gravel around the plants to cover the soil.

7. Water the plants sparingly, a few tablespoons at a time, every two weeks. An eyedropper works well for watering, too. If your book is fairly thick, you can make the planting hole deeper and add a bit of gravel at the bottom for drainage.

MODERN ECLECTIC

SO MANY DÉCORS LEAN TOWARDS AN ECLECTIC AESTHETIC – A MIX OF STYLES THAT DON'T FIT NEATLY INTO ANY SINGLE CATEGORY. It's not that people are indecisive and can't seem to choose one definitive style – it's more a sense of, "Why limit myself when there are so many glorious pieces out there?" This is your style if you pair sleek pieces with rough antiques, or fuse traditional cottage elements with offbeat or contemporary colors.

People with a modern eclectic style tend to buy furniture or accessories because they simply love them and can't resist – and they'll find the perfect spot for them when they get home. (We know people who garden this way, too.) Modern eclectic can be whimsical, artsy, even oddball – but it's always interesting and intriguing.

First steps

Because you tend to be drawn to a great variety of styles, take some time to plan ahead. Although we hesitate to use the word "rule" for eclectic people — after all, it's your ability to transcend hard and fast rules that has brought you to this chapter — we'd like to offer a few "guidelines" to help you create an indoor garden that looks pulled together and cohesive.

Tropical plants in a contemporary vertical treatment

If you adhere to a color scheme, it will make it possible to use items that seemingly have no relation to one another. You can mix styles of furniture, and even differently patterned fabrics by keeping them in the same color family.

A mix of textures gives a rich depth to your décor, even if it's in a singular subtle color, like taupe or slate. If you choose to use neutrals, be sure to add a pop of color here and there, to avoid a ho-hum look. Modern eclectic should never make you yawn. Create your color pop with contrasting pillows on a sofa, a floor rug in an interesting shade (or pattern), or window treatments – all places where you can give your décor some energy.

Succulent assortment

Balancing a varied plant grouping with neutral-toned containers

Conversely, neutrals can help balance things out when there's too much color or a lot of design elements going on. These principles work with plants and their containers, too.

Using high contrast to achieve a pop of energy

97

The Unifying Guideline

You'll find that your indoor plant décor can be both style-defying *and* stylish if you choose one or two colors to highlight, or similar container shapes to collect. Focus on a design element like form, color, texture or shape when gathering your plant, container and accessory materials; it will instantly pull your look together. Love every single type of plant, from cactus to fern? No problem – just plant them in similar warm-hued containers. Can't get enough of all the creative containers you see at the nursery? Pair them with your succulent collection or a wide assortment of airy ferns.

What makes modern eclectic fun when it comes to choosing plants is that you can draw from a wide variety — ferns, palms, succulents, tillandsias, ivies. You name it, it will "go." Since an eclectic décor makes use of a medley of styles, holding the number of plants in a single room to a very carefully chosen few will help keep everything from looking too chaotic.

Simplify

If you find any of this pre-planning too cumbersome or you truly can't be limited to reigning in your design choices, all is not lost. You're not destined to be nominated for hoarding shows if you keep one thing in mind: edit. If you have to have a little bit of everything, that's fine, just avoid having *a lot* of everything. You know about the accessories rule of thumb in fashion, to look in the mirror and remove one item before you leave the house? Modern Eclectics will do well to look around their homes and remove a few things before calling it good.

Plants for a Modern Eclectic Interior

Using these plants will give your décor a decidedly modern feel to it:

African violet (*Saintpaulia ionantha*)
Agave (*Agave* spp.*)
Aloe (*Aloe* spp.)
Bromeliads
Cacti
Cast iron plant (*Aspidistra eliator*)
Coleus (*Solenostemon scutellarioides*)
Croton (*Codiaeum variegatum*)
Desert rose (*Adenium obesum*)
Devil's backbone (*Euphorbia tithymaloides*)
Dracaena (*Dracaena* spp.)
Ferns
Herbs
Ivies
Kangaroo fern (*Microsorum pustulatum*)
Orchids
Palms
Philodendron (*Philodendron* spp.)
Pothos (*Epipremnum aureum*)
Snake plant (*Sansevieria* spp.)
Spider plant (*Chlorophytum comosum*)
Succulents
Tillandsias
ZZ plant (*Zamioculcas zamiifolia*)

Tillandsias in a small aerium

Colorful succulents
set off by identical containers

Potted evergreens mix it up

103

Do This, Not That: Even though eclectic by definition means that you *like* a little bit of everything, you can't really *have* a little bit of everything, because honestly, where would you put it all anyway? You still need to keep basic design principles in mind.

Step-By-Step: Succulent Wreath

Materials

- 2 open wire wreath forms, available at craft stores in the floral department
- Decorative moss, green or gray
- Succulent potting soil
- Floral wire
- An assortment of small 4" potted succulents — choose a variety of colors, sizes and textures. We like *Sempervivum, Sedum, Aeonium, Echeveria, Kalanchoe,* baby toes, and jade plant.
- Chopsticks
- Scissors
- Small brush or spray bottle

1. Lay one wreath form flat on your work surface, and line the inside of it with moss.

2. Carefully spoon in potting soil on top of the moss around the ring of the wreath, mounding it up a bit in the center.

3. Cover with another layer of moss and add the second wire wreath form over it, using 3" lengths of floral wire to tie the two forms together.

4. Carefully make holes through the moss and into the soil for planting — use chopsticks or any small tool to work between the frames of the wire wreath.

5. Gently remove succulents from their pots, separating them out into several smaller plants each, when possible. Tap off the excess soil around the roots, and begin planting the succulents through the moss and into the soil; continue until the top and edges of your wreath are covered.

6. Add bits of moss in-between succulents to keep them in place.

7. Use the brush or spray from the water bottle to remove soil from the moss and plants.

Care and Maintenance

Keep the wreath flat for at least a week, or up to 2-3 weeks, until the succulents have established their roots in the wreath. You can keep the wreath flat on a table for a centerpiece with a candle in the middle, or you can hang it on a door using a wreath hanger.

Keep it out of direct sunlight, but by a brightly lit window, as most succulents need adequate light to maintain their colors. Use a spray bottle to mist it several times a week, and on occasion (about every 2-3 weeks), take it outside and soak it in a small tub of water. Don't overwater these or any other succulents, as they will quickly rot.

HABERDASHERY

OKAY, GUYS. LET'S TALK ABOUT YOUR UNIQUELY MASCULINE SPACE. We hate to stereotype anyone, but if you're like most men, you want your living quarters to be hip, yet comfortable, and you don't want a lot of frou-frou. You might confidently wear a pink shirt on occasion, but the colors you live with likely don't veer in that direction. And we're betting you have better things to do with your time than clean house and fuss over your potted plants.

Giant taro

Lizard tail

Leathers, woods, metallics, and neutral colors suggest masculinity, but a pop of color here and there guards against monotony. Favorite pieces are those that serve a purpose as well as being good-looking, such as the end table that has a magazine pocket attached to the side.

You probably want your plants to fit that description too, don't you? Low- or no-care is a must and architectural plants work well for you. While you want your plants to make a statement, they need to stay out of your way.

Mistletoe cactus

First steps

Dainty doesn't do it when it comes to plant choices, so the containers they're in should have some heft to them. Glazed ceramics, beautiful woods, hypertufa and concrete, metallic pots, and heavy glass will complement their surroundings.

Large floor plants with strong architecture can be like a piece of furniture if given a place of prominence, or they can provide the perfect backdrop for existing pieces.

Split-leaf philodendron

Snake plant

Chinese evergreen

Some men like flowers, and a cut bouquet often fulfills that need, rather than a plant with roots. But for an ongoing color fix at a lower overall cost, consider a potted plant with simple flowers, such as the peace lily *(Spathiphyllum cochlearispathum)* – or even brightly colored foliage like a red or pink Chinese evergreen *(Aglaonema)*.

Assortment of succulents

You might think there aren't that many plants that will forgive you if you get busy with other things and forget to water them or to raise the blinds in the morning to let more of the day's light in. But not all houseplants are needy or demand more of your attention than you're willing to give them. Low-light plants, such as snake plant and ZZ plant and many succulents, will work with rather than against your lifestyle.

Some plants have a coolness factor that appeals to men, such as air plants (tillandsia), which don't need soil to survive. Lithops look just like little rocks – in fact, are called "living stones." Crotons have such vivid colors that they almost don't look real, but it can be just the right plant to provide visual variety. Don't shy away from plants like orchids just because they seem

Euphorbia

so exotic and "flowery" – their strong shape and low maintenance make them perfect for manly spaces. Choose a white bloom color and pair it with an earthy or neutral container color to cut down on the feminine while boosting the masculine appeal.

Plants for a Haberdashery Interior

Agave (*Agave* spp.)

Aloe (*Aloe* spp.)

Arrowhead vine (*Syngonium podophyllum*)

Bromeliads

Cacti

Cast iron plant (*Aspidistra elatior*)

Chinese evergreen (*Aglaonema* spp.)

Corn plant (*Dracaena marginata*)

Croton (*Codiaeum variegatum*)

Donkey ears (*Kalanchoe gastonis-bonnieri*)

Echeveria (*Echeveria* spp.)

Fiddle leaf fig (*Ficus lyrata*)

Jade plant (*Crassula ovata*)

Living stones (*Lithops* spp.)

Orchids

Peace lily (*Spathiphyllum cochlearispathum*)

Philodendron (*Philodendron* spp.)

Pothos (*Epipremnum aureum*)

Rubber tree (*Ficus elastica*)

Snake plant (*Sansevieria* spp.)

Spider plant (*Chlorophytum comosum*)

ZZ plant (*Zamioculcas zamiifolia*)

Donkey ears

Echeveria

Bamboo muhly

Do This, Not That: When it comes to plant choices, it's easy to be swayed by a plant's visual appeal without regard to what happens when you get it home. If you aren't familiar with a particular plant that you're considering purchasing, read the plant tag or ask a store employee what kind of care the plant will require and choose accordingly.

Step-by-Step Project: *Twig Planter*

Here's a really easy project that gives a rugged, natural look to a plain old pot for planting.

Materials

Plain plastic or clay pot – the less tapered, the better
Hot glue gun and glue sticks
Various twigs from the landscape
Pruners or small hand saw

Take a look around your yard (or a friend's, if you don't have a yard) and find some trees or shrubs that have small branches that are able to be pruned. The diameter of the branches can vary, but they should be close in diameter for best results. Look for colorful branches, such as those from a red or yellow twig dogwood, that exhibit brilliant color in fall and winter.

Cut the branches to a length that measures half an inch or so longer than the height of the pot.

Apply a strip of hot glue down the length of each twig and hold it in place on the side of the pot until the glue cools.

Starfish plant

Practical Matters
Care and Feeding of Your Plants

As we confessed right from the start, we kill houseplants. If you're a gardener of any type, it's going to happen, so check your feelings of guilt and inadequacy at the door and forge ahead.

Decorating with houseplants isn't like buying a lamp or a chair. Plants are living things, and just like human beings, they will behave in unpredictable ways and sometimes not follow the rules. But this is what keeps boredom at bay; you'll learn more about their personalities as time goes on.

Your success at growing plants inside needs to match your lifestyle as well as your aesthetics. If you're someone whose every spare minute is filled with activities, it's doubtful that you're going to want to spend a lot of time fussing over your plants (unless growing houseplants happens to be high on your list of extra-curriculars). No matter how you spend the hours in your day, plant selection will be a determining factor in your success.

To simplify your selection process, we've assembled a list of houseplants in a convenient chart, showcasing their characteristics according to the care required to keep them happiest. This is meant to be only a general guide and you should consult the plant tag or your garden center for detailed information about growing a particular plant. They're listed alphabetically, according to common name, but do take note of their botanical names, since sometimes the same common name can be used for two entirely different plants.

For houseplant veterans, you will notice that most of the plants we list are familiar and common. We've done this for a reason. There are other books that suggest more unusual plants for indoor growing, but one of our main objectives is not just to pair up plants with a particular design style, but also to suggest ones that are readily available and fairly easily grown. We want you to be successful in your houseplant endeavors!

For those who may want a bit more of a challenge, we included some that tend to be prima donnas, if you're into that. We happen to think that sometimes a plant really is worth fussing over. And Murphy's Law #728 is that some of you will be able to grow notoriously temperamental plants successfully with no effort at all, yet you can't grow a snake plant to save your life. Just remember: it doesn't mean you're a failure if you kill a plant on occasion. It happens.

Plants denoted with an asterisk (★) are known air purifiers. Plants naturally take carbon dioxide from the air and produce oxygen, but many also remove toxins such as benzene, formaldehyde, toluene and ammonia through a process known as phytoremediation. In fact, some plants are known to remove as much as 85% of a room's toxins in 24 hours. Grow plants for beauty and health!

Houseplants at a Glance

EASY BREEZY

		LIGHT	LIKES IT HUMID	WATER	CONTRAINDICATIONS
Agave	Agave spp.	High		Low	Pointed tips, dangerous to children
Aloe	Aloe barbadensis	Moderate		Low	
Arrowhead vine	Syngonium	Low		Moderate	Toxic
Cactus	Various	High		Low	Spiny, dangerous to children
Cast Iron plant	Aspidistra elatior	Low		Low	
Chinese evergreen *	Aglaonema	Low		Moderate	
Clivia	Clivia miniata	Moderate		Low	
Devil's backbone	Euphorbia tithymaloides	High		Low	
Jade plant	Crassula ovata	High		Low	
Kangaroo fern	Microsorum pustulatum	Low	x	Moderate	
Lucky bamboo	Dracaena sanderiana	Low		High	
Peace lily *	Spathiphyllum cochlearispathum	Low		Moderate	Toxic
Philodendron *	Philodendron cordata	Moderate		Moderate	
Ponytail palm *	Beaucarnea recurvata	High		Low	
Pothos	Epipremnum aureum	Low		Moderate	Toxic
Rabbit's foot fern *	Davallia fejeensis	Moderate	x	High	
Rubber plant	Ficus elastica	High		Moderate	Toxic sap
Sago palm	Cycas revoluta	High		Moderate	Toxic
Snake plant *	Sansevieria trifasciata	Low		Low	Toxic
Spider plant *	Chlorophytum comosum	Moderate		Moderate	
Thanksgiving/ Christmas cactus	Schlumbergera	Moderate		Low	Toxic
Umbrella plant	Schefflera arboricola	High		Moderate	Toxic
Wax plant	Hoya carnosa	Moderate		Moderate	Toxic
ZZ plant *	Zamioculcas zamiifolia	Low		Low	Toxic

MODERATELY MANAGEABLE

		LIGHT	LIKES IT HUMID	WATER	CONTRAINDICATIONS
African violet	*Saintpaulia ionantha*	Moderate	x	Moderate	Sensitive to watering
Bird's nest fern *	*Asplenium nidus*	Moderate	x	Moderate	
Bromeliad *	Various	Low	x	Low	
Caladium	*Caladium*	Low		Moderate	
Canela™ or Cinnamon plant	*Cinnamomum verum*	Moderate		Moderate	
China doll *	*Radermachera sinica*	Moderate		Moderate	
Corn plant *	*Dracaena fragrans*	High		Moderate	
Croton	*Codiaeum variegatum*	High		Moderate	
Desert rose	*Adenium obesum*	High		Low	Mealy bugs
Dumb cane *	*Dieffenbachia*	Moderate		Moderate	Toxic
English ivy *	*Hedera helix*	Moderate		Moderate	Spider mites
Geranium	*Pelargonium* spp.	High		Moderate	
Good Luck plant, Ti plant	*Cordyline fruticosa*	High		Moderate	
Herbs	Various	High		Moderate	
Jasmine	*Jasminus* spp.	High		Moderate	Toxic
Kalanchoe	*Kalanchoe blossfeldiana*	High		Low	Toxic
Money tree	*Pachira aquatica*	High		Low	Toxic
Moth orchid *	*Phalaenopsis*	Low	x	Low	Toxic
Norfolk Island pine	*Araucaria heterophylla*	Moderate	x	Moderate	
Palms	Various	Moderate		High	
Peperomia	*Peperomia* spp.	High		Low	Toxic
Mistletoe cactus	*Rhipsalis* spp.	Moderate		Moderate	Toxic
Taro plant	*Colocasia*	Moderate		High	Toxic
Wandering jew	*Tradescantia zebrina*	Moderate		Moderate	Toxic
Yucca cane	*Yucca guatemalensis*	High		Moderate	Toxic

Houseplants at a Glance

DESIGN DIVAS

		LIGHT	LIKES IT HUMID	WATER	CONTRAINDICATIONS
Boston fern *	*Nephrolepsis exaltata*	Moderate	x	Moderate	Leaf drop
Citrus	Various	High		Moderate	Spider mites
Cyclamen	*Cyclamen persicum*	High		Moderate	Sensitive to watering & temperature
Flamingo flower *	*Anthurium andraeanum*	Moderate	x	Moderate	Sensitive to watering, toxic
Gardenia	*Gardenia jasminoides*	High		Moderate	Pest prone
Lithops	*Lithops* spp.	High		Low	Sensitive to watering
Peacock plant	*Calathea makoyana*	Low		High	Sensitive to watering
Rex begonia	*Begonia rex*	Low	x	Moderate	Sensitive to watering
Rosemary	*Rosemaryinus officinalis*	High	x	Moderate	Leaf drop
String-of-pearls	*Senecio rowleyanus*	Moderate		Low	Sensitive to watering
Weeping fig	*Ficus benjamina*	Moderate		Moderate	Leaf drop

Anthurium

Cyclamen

128

GENERAL CONSIDERATIONS

Planting Soil

Garden centers sell various planting mixes for a reason – different plants like different conditions and you want to mimic a plant's natural environment as much as possible. For example, since cacti grow in hot, dry areas of the world where fast-draining sand is the soil standard, you wouldn't want to plant one in the heavy clay soil from your garden. That would be sabotaging your success right from the start. It might do fine for a while, but eventually the cactus would decline and die. (Actually, most plants would die if you planted them in clay soil in a pot. It would be like sticking someone's head in a plastic bag and expecting them to be able to breathe.)

Take advantage of the plant-specific soil mixes that are available: orchid, cacti and succulents, African violet, etc. When you get to know plants and the conditions they need to thrive, you'll learn that the specialty mixes can sometimes be used for plants other than the ones listed on the label, too. The biggest consideration for potting mixes is drainage. Water needs to be able to drain away and unlike plants that grow outside in the ground, plants in containers have a pretty confined space. Unless the plant actually likes soggy feet, poor drainage can be a death knell.

Mind Your Drainage

Containers play a big part in the overall fashion sense of your display. In fact, the container may be the single most influential piece of the scene you create, or at least as important as the plant itself. Think of it in the way that you yourself dress for different types of situations –

sometimes you wear formal clothing and other times your jeans are the couture du jour.

As we've seen, using non-traditional pieces to stand in for planters creates a much more interesting and unique (as well as inexpensive) indoor garden, but it can also invite issues and problems with drainage. Be careful to not prioritize creativity over practicality; the most successful gardens, inside and out, have both in equal balance. After all, we're talking about living, breathing plant material here, not stagnant artifacts. Be aware of the drainage needs for your particular plants, and be prepared to alter your creative container choices to support that plant life.

- **Use cachepots.** A cachepot is a container – any container – without drainage holes. Simply place your plant, in its nursery pot, inside the more decorative container without repotting. You can water plants in the cachepot, but be sure to empty any standing water fairly quickly to avoid rotting. Most plants thrive well when displayed in cachepots, making this a very versatile option.

- **Drill holes.** Plants planted directly into pots without drainage holes usually need a hole drilled in order to avoid rotting. Ceramic, glass, wood and metal containers can be easily altered with the correct drill bit. For metal or steel, use titanium or cobalt bits; for glass, use tungsten carbide spear-tipped drill bits and diamond-tipped drill bits; for wood, ground tungsten carbide or diamond tips, and regular drill bits. Using the wrong drill bit will either destroy the bit or the piece you are drilling into, so if you're in doubt, take your container into the hardware store and seek advice.

- **Match pot to plant.** Sometimes a plant will love the conditions of the pot you love, and if not, you'll need to closely monitor your watering in order for the plant to thrive. Succulents will do well in most types of containers, but if yours doesn't have a drainage hole (teacup, mug or barware, for example), simply water very sparingly (one or two tablespoons at a time). Alternatively, plants like button ferns and baby's tears love to have some extra moisture and likely won't complain as long as they are not simply sitting in water. Do a little experimenting after first knowing your plants' peculiarities.

Common Houseplant Pest Problems

When we say common, we don't mean that you are absolutely going to have a plethora of plant pest problems just because you grow plants in the house. But if you do, it's most likely to be these.

Fungus gnats

If there's one insect that nearly every grower of houseplants has encountered, it's the fungus gnat. They're very tiny and black, they don't make any noise, and they don't bite. Only in severe infestations is it a problem for the plant itself, but these little black guys can be mildly annoying when you're sitting there in front of the television and you swear you've got a floater in your eye.

Generally a problem caused by overwatering, controlling fungus gnats is relatively simple. Stop overwatering! With some exceptions, allowing the potting medium in which your plants are growing to become dry down to about an inch below the surface before the next watering will discourage fungus gnats from setting up housekeeping.

Mealy bugs

These fuzzy white insects have their favorite plants to attack, including orchids, citrus, ferns, cacti and gardenias. They will resemble tiny bits of cotton and can be found on the undersides of leaves and in the crevices of these plants. Only the females do damage, as they are the only ones to suck plant juices. The males only exist to fertilize the females!

Whitefly

You'll know you have whiteflies when you touch your plant and a small cloud of teeny white bugs starts flying about. Whiteflies generally stay on the underneath sides of plant leaves, where they lay their eggs and tap into a leaf's juices for their dinner. In their wake, they leave a sticky substance called honeydew. You might even see some of the honeydew on the table or floor beneath infected plants.

Aphids

These guys come in various color assortments, but with houseplants, you're most likely to see the green ones. They're tiny, clear-winged insects and they love to feed on a plant's new growth. They too, leave honeydew in their wake. You won't see them flying about, even though they have wings; they'll be lethargically crawling on the ends of stems where new leaves form – and sucking the life out of them.

Scale

These sucking insects don't even look like live beings. They look like barnacles, attached to the leaves and stems of your plants. But don't be fooled! They're very much alive and living off your plant's life blood. These are the most difficult to remove and since as adults they have a somewhat hard shell to protect them, they'll be the most resistant to chemical products meant to kill them.

What to do

We like to take an organic approach to controlling pests, so our recommendations are just that, even if it's to cut your losses and compost the plant. Win some, lose some. In any case, at the first sign of a problem, isolate the affected plant so that it doesn't spread the love to its housemates.

In the case of flying pests, sticky traps will help. Placing them in your pots will catch the majority of them and cut down on new generations. A small hand vacuum can be used to suck them up, too. Sometimes all that's needed is to take the plant outside or to the bathroom shower and gently spray it with water to remove the pests, although this won't work for scale. You'll need to pick those off manually.

If things have gotten too out of hand, neem oil-based products can help you regain control of most problematic and persistent pests. Your garden center can help you out with specific product recommendations.

Feed Me!

Because houseplants have very limited resources from which to gather nutrients, it's important to provide them on an ongoing basis. Besides the plants themselves using the nutrients in their planting medium, regular watering flushes some away over time. There are many houseplant fertilizers on the market, including some that are made especially for specific types of plants, such as African violets. As with pest control, we prefer organic methods of feeding and there are several options available that will provide important nutrients with regular use.

Compost teas, fish emulsions, and worm castings are just a few of the choices you have. Your local garden center can help you find what you need. Keep this tip in mind though: In winter, many plants will slow their growth and may even enter a dormant period. Withhold feeding until you see signs of active growth, then resume a regular schedule.

Plant Heroics

Just like in your outdoor gardens, plants sometimes live longer than they should. While many are long-lived, there are those that look like they should be put out of their misery after performing well for several years. This is normal.

But if you're like us, you hate to throw out anything that has a hint of life left in it. You know the ones – they've lost their lower leaves and look like lollipops in a pot. Or they suffer from perpetual wilt, but they might perk up, right?

Of course, some plants do recover from such maladies, but if after a reasonable time – say, a month or so – your straggler still isn't showing signs of recovery, just bite the bullet and compost it. Think of it as a chance to try something new.

Here Kitty, Kitty!

Pets can prove to be a challenge for many houseplant growers. Cats, in particular, seem to love chewing on greens, especially if they resemble grass. Besides disfiguring your plants, they might be ingesting something toxic to them. The ASPCA posts a list on their website (http://www.aspca.org) of the most common toxic plants (397 for cats, 392 for dogs) – but not all of those are suitable as houseplants. And they vary in their toxicity, depending on how much is ingested.

They also list those plants that are known to be non-toxic for cats and dogs, and there are many more of those. To be absolutely safe, either grow only those known to be non-toxic, or place your houseplants out of reach of Puff and Spot.

Keeping It Real (or not)

Okay, if we must...

There are still those of you who insist that you have a brown thumb and kill everything. If you plant murderers are reading this book, we applaud you. While we are fairly certain that there's at least one plant we mention here that even you can't kill, we would be remiss if we didn't at least mention that there is another option. At the risk of committing horticultural blasphemy, you can always "grow" artificial plants.

We like the real thing, of course, but there are some pretty amazing replicas out there. If you're going to go this route, for heaven's sake, buy quality plants that truly look realistic. If you want the effect without the worry of committing plant homicide, be willing to spend a little more since you'll have them for a very long time. Forever, even.

Fabulous faux-ever

135

Acknowledgments

WRITING A BOOK IS HARD WORK. Even for two people who have been writing for a while now (and thoroughly enjoying it), you'd think that eventually we would get used to meeting deadlines, suffering from writer's block, and life just generally getting in the way. But there were some days when we wondered what we'd gotten ourselves into.

A book is never just the product of its writers, of course. It is a group effort by editors, graphic artists, and a publisher. It is nourished by the experience gleaned over the years from friends and colleagues, sometimes found in the most unlikely of places. The end result has been helped along the way by people who shouldn't even care at all – yet they did – and they came to our aid when we needed it. Many went above and beyond the call of duty, and we are grateful.

At the risk of forgetting someone (that always happens, doesn't it?), we'd like to try to mention those who played a part in making *Indoor Plant Décor* a reality, whether it was by providing us with materials or a location for a photo shoot, photos themselves, ideas to include in the book, deadline extensions from our other employers, and perhaps most importantly, support and encouragement that we could actually pull this off.

The list is long: Debra Lee Baldwin, Provencal Home in Austin, Catherine Jones, Diane Blazek, Garden Media Group (Suzi McCoy, Stacey Silvers, Katie Dubow), Theresa Loe, Rebecca Sweet, Susan Morrison, Katie Elzer-Peters, Laura Livengood, Jayme Jenkins, Pam Penick, Charlotte Germane, Louise Hartwig (Thanks, Mom!), DGS (you know who you are!), and the passengers on planes and other various strangers who had to listen to us as we shared the excitement of writing a book.

Special thanks to P. Allen Smith for what he does for the gardening world in general and for sharing his expertise with both of us personally, which has helped us grow as gardeners. His endorsement on the back cover of our book means the world to us. Many, many thanks to The Great Outdoors Garden Center and Nursery in Austin and its fabulous staff, who lent us an uncommon amount of plants and accessories for our photo shoots. Your generosity and cheerfulness were epic.

To our significant others – Roman Baumle and Brett Davis: We're sorry. We really are. You had to endure the messed up home life that comes with long hours, missed family events, being ignored, leftovers (if you were lucky), short tempers, and whining when things weren't going right. You hung in there, for better or worse, and we know that you had nothing to gain from it except to help make our dream come true. You have been the best cheerleaders two women could ever have. We love you.

The family at St. Lynn's Press — and you truly feel like family — has been more than we could ask for in ways that simply can't be numbered. For first time authors, the learning curve is steep and you made the journey from start to end as enjoyable as it could possibly be. To Paul Kelly, we owe such gratitude for the genuine thoughtfulness and caring that you have for the people who enter your life. We feel blessed that we are two of them and that we somehow managed to get you to say yes. You have the patience of a saint and we wish you could teach the world. To Cathy Dees, whose sense of humor matches ours (squee!), you've been a joy to work with and we're indebted to you for what Paul calls "working your magic." Holly Rosborough, your graphic talents seem to flow from you as naturally as breathing. All we had to do was ask for something and with lightning speed, you obliged. Everything looked better after you got done with it.

We would be remiss if we didn't thank those of you who took the time to buy and/or read our book. No matter what you think of it, we know that it took a bit of your time and we don't take that lightly. Our hope is that you found something of value that will enrich your home and your indoor garden.

Kylee — Jenny

One more thing...

From Kylee: Jenny, we were friends before we started on this book-writing adventure and we're even better friends now. In life, just as in the book, we complement each other in all the right ways. Though I'm rarely at a loss for words, there are times when I don't need any because you just know. Like now. Love you always.

From Jenny: Writing a book with your dearest friend while going through treatment for breast cancer was an adventure I can't quite believe we undertook – but one that I am deeply grateful for! Kylee, my profound thanks for your energy, encouragement, humor and cheerfulness, but most of all, for your faith that this could be done. I owe you a huge bag of Rolos and a case of diet Mountain Dew.

PHOTO & DESIGN CREDITS

The authors gratefully acknowledge the following for permission to use their images.

RESOURCES

PLANTS

Logee's Greenhouses, Ltd.
http://www.logees.com
141 North Street
Danielson, Connecticut 06239
Phone: (888) 330-8038

Moss and Stone Gardens
http://www.mossandstonegardens.com
Raleigh, North Carolina
Phone: (919) 622-4150

Kartuz Greenhouses
http://www.kartuz.com
P.O. Box 790
Vista, California 92085
Phone: (760) 941-3613

Almost Eden
http://almostedenplants.com
1240 Smith Road
Merryville, Louisiana 70653
Phone: (337) 375-2114

Stokes Tropicals
http://stokestropicals.plants.com
4806 E. Old Spanish Trail
Jeanerette, Louisiana 70544
Phone: (800) 624-9706

Glasshouse Works
http://www.glasshouseworks.com
P.O. Box 97
Stewart, Ohio 45778
Phone: (740) 662-2142

Living Stones Nursery
http://lithops.net
2936 N. Stone
Tucson, Arizona 85705
Phone: (520) 628-8773

CONTAINERS & PLANTERS

Independent Garden Centers

H. Potter (www.hpotter.com), feat. on pp. 9-10

Woolly Pocket (www.woollypocket.com)

The Growers Exchange
 (www.thegrowers-exchange.com)

Chive (www.chive.com)

West Elm

IKEA

T.J. Maxx and Marshall's

Lowe's, Home Depot, and other chain stores

Goodwill, garage sales, thrift shops, flea markets

FOR FURTHER READING

The Houseplant Expert, by D.G. Hessayon

The Unexpected Houseplant, by Tovah Martin

The Complete Houseplant Survival Manual: Essential Know-How for Keeping (Not Killing) More Than 160 Indoor Plants, by Barbara Pleasant

Succulent Container Gardens: Design Eye-Catching Displays with 350 Easy-Care Plants, by Debra Lee Baldwin

Logee's Greenhouses Spectacular Container Plants: How to Grow Dramatic Flowers for Your Patio, Sunroom, Windowsill, and Outdoor Spaces, by Byron E. Martin and Laurelynn G. Martin

The Complete Guide to Keeping Your Houseplants Alive and Thriving: Everything You Need to Know Explained Simply, by Sandy Baker

Terrarium Craft: Create 50 Magical, Miniature Worlds, by Amy Bryant Aiello and Kate Bryant

The Complete Practical Encyclopedia of Bonsai: The essential step-by-step guide to creating, growing, and displaying bonsai, by Ken Norman

Nerve plant

ONLINE PLANT INFORMATION

MOBOT (Missouri Botanical Garden): http://www.missouribotanicalgarden.org/gardens-gardening/your-garden/plant-finder.aspx

Dave's Garden: http://www.davesgarden.com

USDA Plants Database: http://plants.usda.gov

National Gardening Association: http://www.garden.org/plantfinder

Better Homes and Gardens: http://www.bhg.com/gardening/plant-dictionary/houseplant

Guide to Houseplants: http://www.guide-to-houseplants.com/index.html

Costa Farms: http://www.costafarms.com/public/plantlibrary.aspx

About the Authors

Kylee Baumle enjoys photographing gardens as much as she does tending to them. Her photos have been published in trade catalogs and garden magazines and have been featured in several gardening books. Kylee writes for a number of gardening publications, including *Horticulture* magazine, where she is also Book Review Editor. She has a weekly local newspaper column on gardening and has appeared on America's Web Radio show, America's Homegrown Veggies, Gardening Today and Garden World Report. She's also been a guest host on the popular #gardenchat on Twitter.

Kylee, who also is a dental hygienist, lives on an acre in rural Northwest Ohio farm counry with her husband Roman, several cats, and enjoys gardening both inside and out. She writes about her growing experiences on her award-winning blog, Our Little Acre (www.ourlittleacre.com).

Jenny Peterson is an Austin, Texas-based landscape designer and freelance writer specializing in xeriscaping and small urban spaces. Her design work has been featured in *Garden Up!* (Cool Springs Press, 2011) on vertical gardening, in *Small-Space Container Gardens* (Timber Press, 2012), as well as in *Horticulture* and *Cottages & Bungalows* magazines. She is a member of the renowned Garden Designers Roundtable, a nationwide group of landscape designers who blog monthly about all aspects of gar-

den design, and has appeared several times on The Central Texas Gardener, a long-running public television garden program.

Jenny also writes on her blog, J. Peterson Garden Design (www.jpetersongardendesign.com), and is a regional writer for Houzz.com, a popular site for interior and exterior design. For several years, she was a small-space dweller, gardening on a 150-square-foot, windy third-story balcony. She now lives in a house on a full acre, with lots of room for indoor and outdoor plants.

Come visit us on Facebook at Indoor Plant Décor, and at www.IndoorPlantDecor.com.